RACE CAR DRIVERS

by David West

illustrated by Peter Wilks *and* Geoff Ball

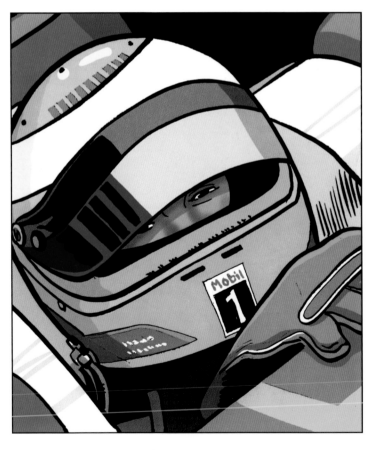

New York

Published in 2008 by The Rosen Publishing Group, Inc.
29 East 21st Street, New York, NY 10010

First edition, 2008

Designed and produced by
David West Books

Editor: Gail Bushnell

Photo credits:
5br, Rechlin; 6-7t, Dan Smith; 6-7m, Imperial Assassin; 6-7b, U.S. Air Force photo by Larry McTighe; 7t, Rick Dikeman; 7m, Evil moe; 44-5, CIK/FIA Press releases GFDL.

Library of Congress Cataloging-in-Publication Data

West, David, 1956-
  Race car driver / by David West ; illustrated by Peter Wilks and
Geoff Ball. -- 1st ed.
     p. cm. -- (Graphic careers)
  Includes index.
  ISBN 978-1-4042-1452-1 (library binding) -- ISBN 978-1-4042-1453-8
(pbk.) -- ISBN 978-1-4042-1454-5 (6 pack)
 1. Automobile racing. 2. Automobile racing drivers. I. Wilks,
Peter, ill. II. Ball, Geoff, ill. III. Title.
  GV1029.W43 2007
  796.72--dc22
                                          2007045174

Manufactured in China

CONTENTS

EARLY YEARS OF CAR RACING

On December 19, 1893, the French news magazine *Le Petit Journal* announced a trial for "horseless carriages" from Paris to Rouen. Twenty-one vehicles took part in the event in 1894, and although it was not a race it ignited interest in automobiles.

Panhard-Levassor, *1895*

Fernand Gabriel driving a Mors in the Paris-Madrid 1903 race, which was stopped when eight people were killed and many more injured during the first day.

THE FIRST RACE

After the success of the Paris-Rouen trial, it was thought that a race would be more exciting. Thus the first organized car race was held in 1895 on the open roads of France, from Paris to Bordeaux and back. Emile Levassor won the race in a *Panhard-Levassor* that had a top speed of 18.5 miles (29.7 kilometers) per hour.

BIGGER AND FASTER

These early racing events were both a proving ground for the new car makes and a shop window for people wanting to buy cars. Winning was all-important. Speeds increased as engine sizes grew. By 1908, massive engines of 12–13 liters, mounted on flimsy frames with only primitive brakes, propelled the cars up to 100 miles (160 kilometers) per hour.

A Bentley charges round the Le Mans 24-hour race circuit. The race tested a car's reliability as well as its speed.

INTERNATIONAL CAR RACING

Car racing became a major international sporting event when, in 1900, James Gordon Bennett, an American newspaper tycoon living in Paris, put up the cash and trophy for a series of races promoting a contest between national teams. However, there were many car manufacturers who could not enter due to the three-cars-per-team rule. Inevitably, other race events began to appear. In 1904, William K. Vanderbilt organized a cup in his name in the United States and in 1906, the French held the first Grand Prix at Le Mans.

Start of the 1910 Vanderbilt Cup.

Indianapolis, 1912

THE PURE RACER

By the 1930s the high-priced road cars were transformed into pure racers, with Delage, Auto Union, Mercedes-Benz, and Bugatti constructing streamlined cars with supercharged engines and extensive use of aluminum alloys. Apart from the Italian *Mille Miglia*, most races were now held on specially built tracks such as the Nurburgring in Germany and the Indianapolis 500 in the United States. By the 1950s, car racing events were held around the world, from single-seater (open wheel) to stock car racing, attracting huge crowds who craved the sights, sounds, and smells of speed and danger.

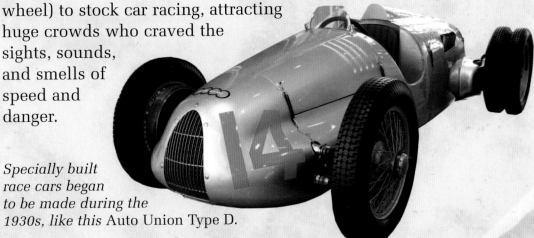

Specially built race cars began to be made during the 1930s, like this Auto Union Type D.

TYPES OF AUTO RACING

Since 1895 car racing has become increasingly popular. As various regulations, formulas, and racing organizations have formed over the years, so have the many variations of the sport.

CATEGORIES

One of the most popular forms of auto racing worldwide is single-seater (open wheel) racing. The best known is Formula One, which has an annual world championship for drivers and constructors. Touring car racing is popular in Europe and the U.S. It uses heavily modified street cars. The most popular form of auto sport in the U.S. is NASCAR. The race cars look like street cars, but underneath the lightweight bodies they are specialized racing machines. Another popular street-type car racing is rallying. The World Rally Championship is the top series, with events taking place all over the world. In sports car racing, specially built prototype cars and production sports cars compete on closed circuits. The most famous races are the 24 Hours of Le Mans and Daytona. One of the noisiest and fastest is drag racing, where two specialized vehicles compete along a quarter-mile (400 meter) strip. These are just a few of the many types of auto racing. Others include Targa Racing (Targa Rally), one-make racing, production car racing, historical racing, and hill climbing.

A Formula One Ferrari takes a bend at Indianapolis (above). GTP sports cars race at Lexington, Ohio (right).

Top methanol dragster at Santa Pod (left).

Henning Solberg drives a Peugeot 206 during the WRC Neste Rally, Finland (above).

NASCAR race cars hurtle around the Daytona 500 oval circuit (left).

JUAN MANUEL FANGIO
FORMULA ONE
THE GREATEST DRIVER OF ALL TIME

IT IS 1990. THE FAMOUS ARGENTINIAN RACING DRIVER FANGIO IS BEING INTERVIEWED ABOUT HIS RACE AT THE NURBURGRING, GERMANY, IN 1957.

THIS WAS THE BIG RACE OF THE YEAR. IF YOU WON THIS YOU WOULD WIN THE CHAMPIONSHIP FOR THE FIFTH TIME.

YES. I WAS STARTING IN POLE POSITION.* THE TWO BRITISH DRIVERS, MIKE HAWTHORN AND PETER COLLINS, WERE BEHIND ME IN THE FERRARIS.

MY MASERATI HAD PIRELLI TIRES, WHICH WERE GOOD FOR GRIP BUT WORE FASTER THAN THE HARDER ENGLEBERTS TIRES THE FERRARIS WERE USING.

THEIR TIRES WOULD ALLOW THEM TO RACE WITHOUT STOPPING IN THE PITS, BUT I WOULD NEED TO CHANGE MY TIRES.

*FIRST POSITION ON THE START GRID.

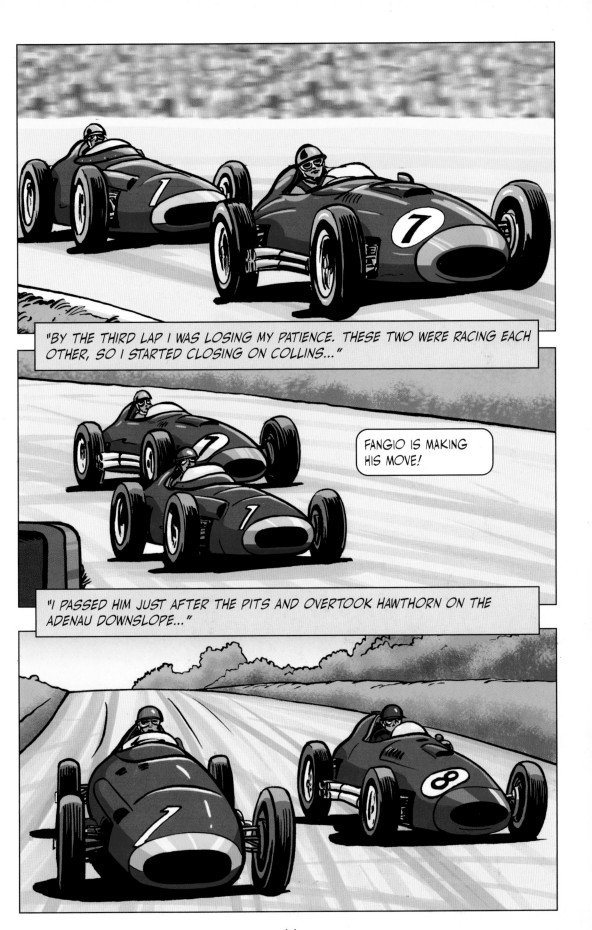

"BY THE THIRD LAP I WAS LOSING MY PATIENCE. THESE TWO WERE RACING EACH OTHER, SO I STARTED CLOSING ON COLLINS..."

FANGIO IS MAKING HIS MOVE!

"I PASSED HIM JUST AFTER THE PITS AND OVERTOOK HAWTHORN ON THE ADENAU DOWNSLOPE..."

FANGIO LEADS HERE AT THE NURBURGRING...

"BY THE FOURTH LAP I WAS CONCENTRATING ON MY PLAN..."

"THE TWO ENGLISH DRIVERS KEPT CLOSE BEHIND, BUT AS THEY KEPT RACING EACH OTHER I WAS ABLE, BIT BY BIT, TO BUILD UP MY THIRTY-SECOND LEAD..."

LOOK AT THAT, SON. FANGIO IS PULLING AWAY FROM THE FERRARIS.

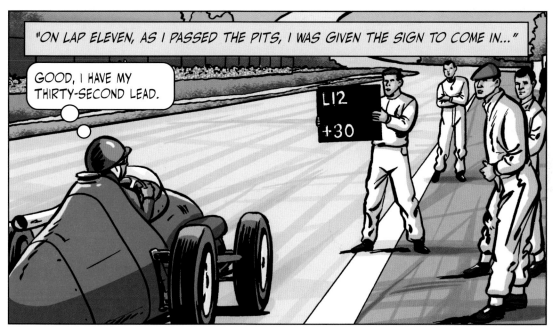

"ON LAP ELEVEN, AS I PASSED THE PITS, I WAS GIVEN THE SIGN TO COME IN..."

GOOD, I HAVE MY THIRTY-SECOND LEAD.

L12 +30

"AND ON LAP TWELVE I PULLED INTO THE PITS..."

WATER! QUICK!

"I WAS SO THIRSTY, I DRANK A WHOLE BOTTLE OF MINERAL WATER. THE MECHANICS CHANGED THE TIRES AND REFUELED THE CAR..."

THE MECHANICS SHOULD HAVE FINISHED BY NOW.

"SUDDENLY I REALIZED SOMETHING WAS WRONG..."

WELL, THAT'S THE END OF A BEAUTIFUL DREAM.

"THE NEW TIRES TOOK A COUPLE OF LAPS TO WARM UP, WHICH MADE ME FIFTY-ONE SECONDS BEHIND..."

"AS THE TIRES BEDDED IN, I FOUND I WAS GAINING GROUND ON THE FERRARIS..."

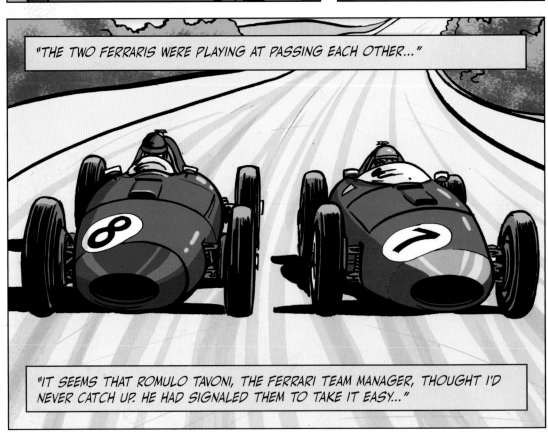

"THE TWO FERRARIS WERE PLAYING AT PASSING EACH OTHER..."

"IT SEEMS THAT ROMULO TAVONI, THE FERRARI TEAM MANAGER, THOUGHT I'D NEVER CATCH UP. HE HAD SIGNALED THEM TO TAKE IT EASY..."

"I REALIZED THAT YOU COULD TAKE SOME BENDS FASTER IN A HIGHER GEAR..."

"IT WAS RISKY..."

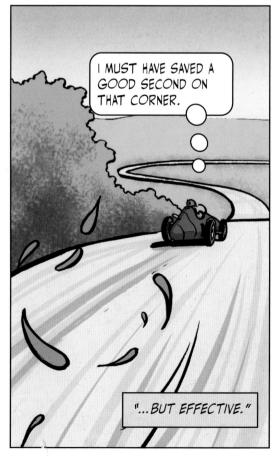

I MUST HAVE SAVED A GOOD SECOND ON THAT CORNER.

"...BUT EFFECTIVE."

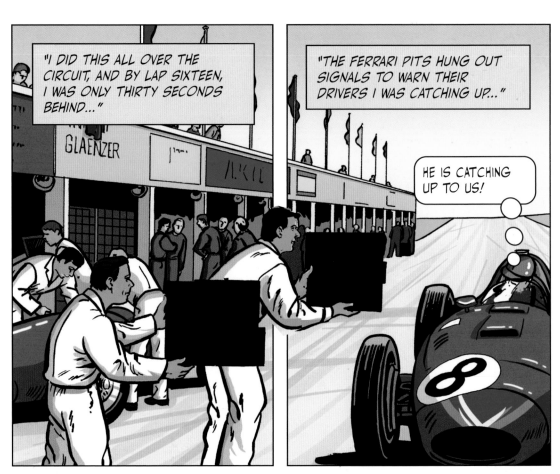

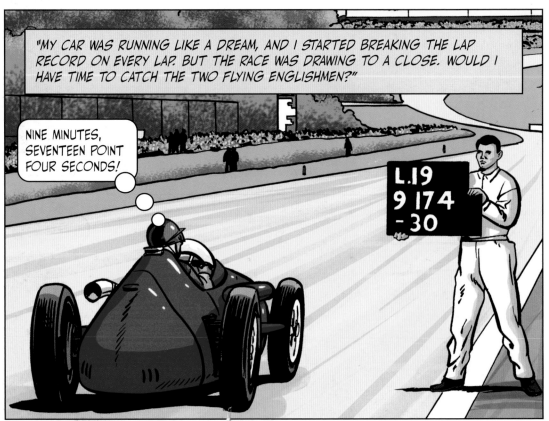

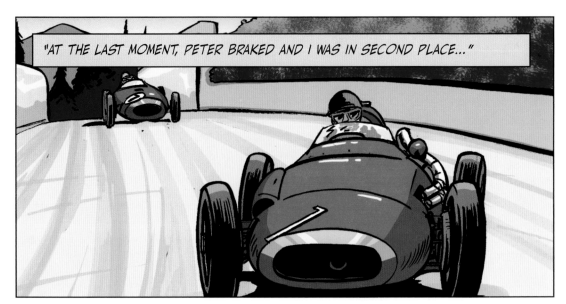

"AT THE LAST MOMENT, PETER BRAKED AND I WAS IN SECOND PLACE..."

"AND THERE WAS HAWTHORN, RIGHT IN FRONT OF ME. HE REALLY PILED IT ON..."

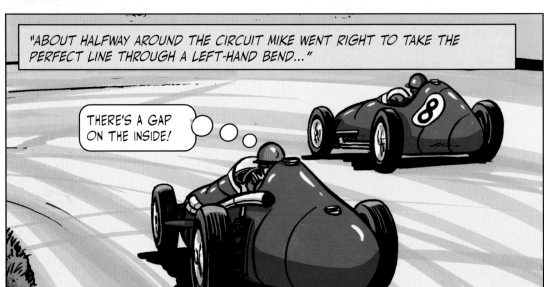

"ABOUT HALFWAY AROUND THE CIRCUIT MIKE WENT RIGHT TO TAKE THE PERFECT LINE THROUGH A LEFT-HAND BEND..."

THERE'S A GAP ON THE INSIDE!

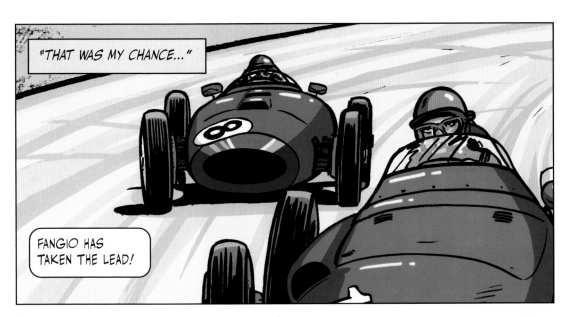

"THAT WAS MY CHANCE..."

FANGIO HAS TAKEN THE LEAD!

"AFTER THAT I REALLY TURNED IT ON. MIKE FOUGHT BACK, AND WHEN I GOT TO THE CHECKERED FLAG HE WAS ONLY THREE SECONDS BEHIND ME."

FANGIO TAKES THE CHECKERED FLAG HERE AT THE NURBURGRING.

FANGIO RETIRED FROM CAR RACING THE NEXT YEAR. HIS RECORD FIVE WORLD CHAMPIONSHIP TITLES STOOD FOR 45 YEARS. TODAY HE IS STILL CONSIDERED BY MANY TO BE THE GREATEST DRIVER OF ALL TIME.   **THE END**

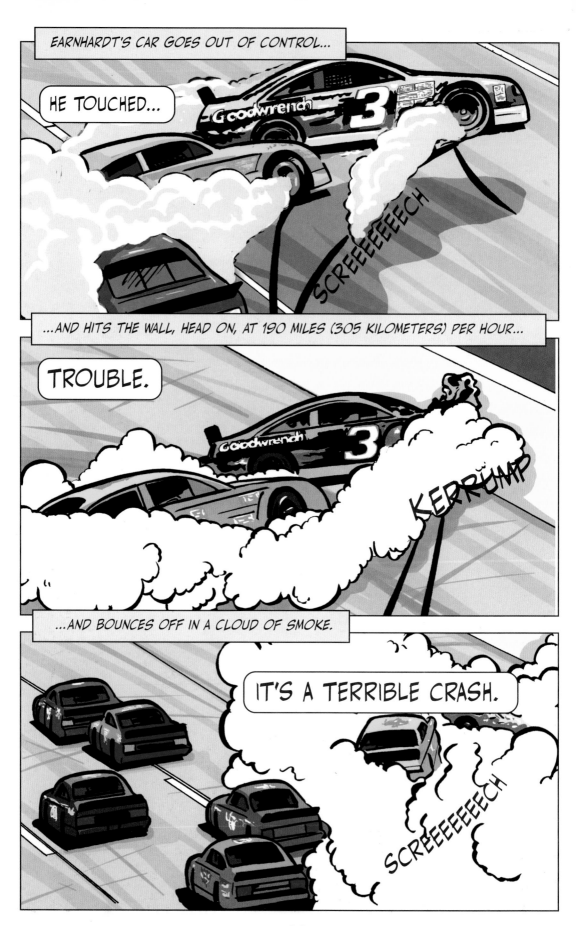

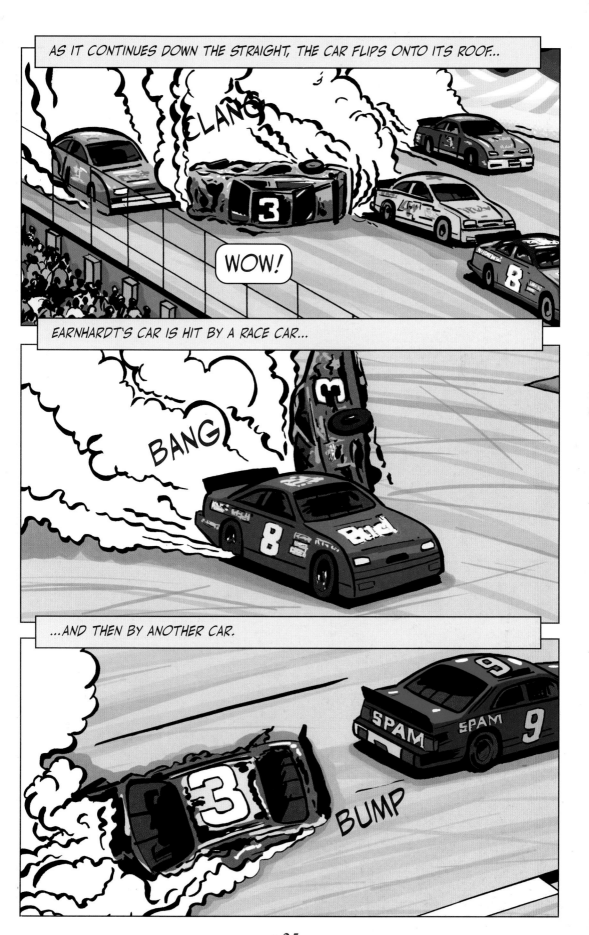

WITHIN SECONDS THE EMERGENCY VEHICLES ARRIVE AT EARNHARDT'S CAR.

EARNHARDT'S NUMBER THREE WENT HEAD ON INTO THE WALL AT ONE HUNDRED AND NINETY MILES PER HOUR!

IT LOOKS LIKE THEY'RE GOING TO HAVE TO CUT HIM OUT OF THE CAR.

CHEVROLET

THE HUSHED CROWD WAITS AS THE RESCUE CREWS WORK TO FREE THE DRIVER.

THEN, TO THE RELIEF OF THE CROWD...

EARNHARDT IS ON HIS FEET, AND HE IS WALKING TO THE AMBULANCE.

HE GIVES THE THUMBS UP TO THE CROWD. THAT IS ONE TOUGH CUSTOMER.

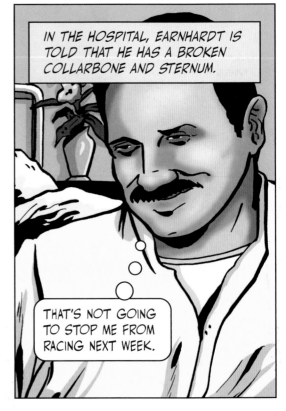

IN THE HOSPITAL, EARNHARDT IS TOLD THAT HE HAS A BROKEN COLLARBONE AND STERNUM.

THAT'S NOT GOING TO STOP ME FROM RACING NEXT WEEK.

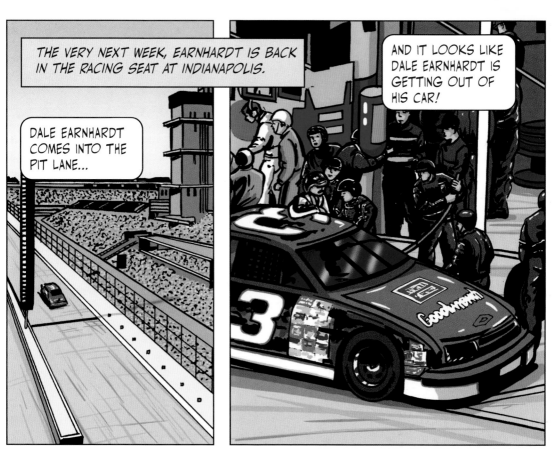

THE NEXT WEEKEND, DALE EARNHARDT CROSSES THE START/FINISH LINE DURING QUALIFICATION AT WATKINS GLEN, NEW YORK.

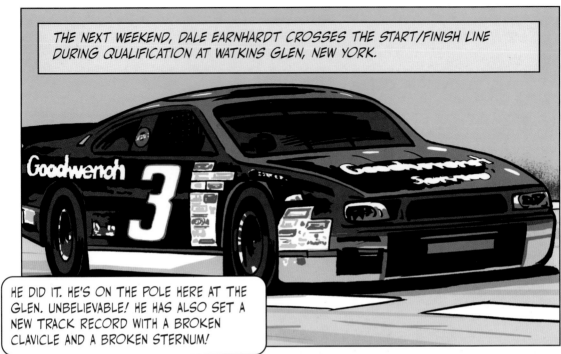

HE DID IT. HE'S ON THE POLE HERE AT THE GLEN. UNBELIEVABLE! HE HAS ALSO SET A NEW TRACK RECORD WITH A BROKEN CLAVICLE AND A BROKEN STERNUM!

ON RACE DAY, DALE EARHARDT FANS WEAR NEWLY PRINTED T-SHIRTS.

ON THE POLE AT THE GLEN
"It hurt so good!"
Dale Earnhardt

WHILE WAITING ON THE TRACK IN HIS CAR, EARNHARDT IS INTERVIEWED.

DALE, IS THIS THE DAY YOU STAY, OR DO YOU COME OUT OF THE CAR?

I'M A LITTLE SORE IN MY SHOULDER RIGHT NOW, BUT WE'LL JUST HAVE TO SEE HOW IT GOES.

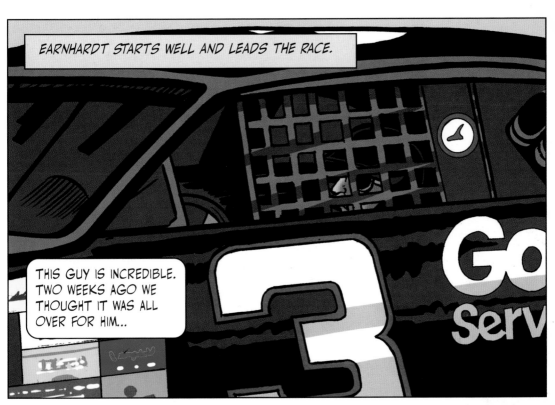

EARNHARDT STARTS WELL AND LEADS THE RACE.

THIS GUY IS INCREDIBLE. TWO WEEKS AGO WE THOUGHT IT WAS ALL OVER FOR HIM...

EARNHARDT LEADS FOR MOST OF THE RACE, BUT THE PAIN WEARS HIM DOWN.

...AND EARNHARDT FINISHES SIXTH.

AT THE END OF THE SEASON, DALE EARNHARDT'S CHAMPIONSHIP POSITION WAS FOURTH. HE WAS NEVER TO ACHIEVE THAT EIGHTH CHAMPIONSHIP WIN. SADLY, HE WAS KILLED FIVE YEARS LATER, IN 2001, IN A CRASH AT THE DAYTONA 500.   **THE END**

LEWIS HAMILTON
FORMULA ONE
ROOKIE DRIVER

IN 1992, A NEWS CREW FROM A CHILDREN'S TV SHOW IS FILMING A REMOTE-CONTROLLED RACE CAR EVENT.

THE WINNER IS A SEVEN-YEAR-OLD NAMED LEWIS HAMILTON.

IT IS THREE YEARS LATER. LEWIS HAS BEEN RACING KARTS, SMALL RACE CARS WITH NO SUSPENSION OR BODYWORK, IN THE SUPER ONE BRITISH CHAMPIONSHIP, FROM THE AGE OF EIGHT. HIS FATHER, ANTHONY, IS HIS MANAGER AND MECHANIC.

IN THE LAST RACE, LEWIS IS CHEERED ON BY HIS FAMILY...

COME ON, LEWIS!

HE TAKES THE CHECKERED FLAG IN FIRST PLACE.

LEWIS FINISHES THE SEASON BY WINNING THE SUPER ONE BRITISH CHAMPIONSHIP IN THE CADET CLASS.

THAT SAME YEAR, LEWIS IS AT THE AUTOSPORT AWARDS.

HE MEETS RON DENNIS, THE FORMULA ONE MCLAREN-MERCEDES TEAM BOSS.

I WANT TO RACE IN FORMULA ONE. CAN I DRIVE FOR YOUR TEAM?

GO AND WIN SOME MORE RACES AND WE'LL SEE.

FROM 1996 TO 1997, LEWIS CONTINUES TO RACE IN KARTS.

THE GOING IS TOUGH. HE HAS TO FIT SCHOOL IN BETWEEN THE BUSY RACE SCHEDULE AND TRAINING.

THERE IS LITTLE TIME TO SPEND WITH HIS FRIENDS. WHEN BULLIES TAKE AN INTEREST IN HIM...

NOBODY WILL BOTHER ME WHEN I BECOME A BLACK BELT.

...HE TAKES UP KARATE.

THE SPORT OF KARTING IS EXPENSIVE TO COMPETE IN. HIS FATHER HAS TO HOLD DOWN THREE JOBS.

WE NEED SOME SPONSORSHIP TO HELP PAY FOR ALL THIS.

BETWEEN 1996 AND 1997, LEWIS WINS FOUR MORE BRITISH KART TITLES.

THE FOLLOWING YEAR, RON DENNIS SIGNS LEWIS, AGED 13, FOR MCLAREN'S DEVELOPMENT PROGRAM.

THERE IS NOW MONEY AND SUPPORT FOR LEWIS IN HIS RACING AND SCHOOLWORK.

WITH MCLAREN BEHIND HIM, LEWIS GOES ON TO WIN THE EUROPEAN KARTING CHAMPIONSHIP IN 2000, AT THE AGE OF 15. IN 2001 HE COMPETES IN THE SUPER-A WORLD KARTING CHAMPIONSHIP, FINISHING 15TH.

IN 2001, LEWIS MOVES INTO SINGLE-SEAT RACE CARS. THE FOLLOWING YEAR HE FINISHES THIRD IN THE FORMULA RENAULT CHAMPIONSHIP.

THIS IS MORE DIFFICULT THAN I FIRST THOUGHT IT WOULD BE!

AT THE NEXT ATTEMPT, HE WINS THE TITLE.

THIS IS MORE LIKE IT!

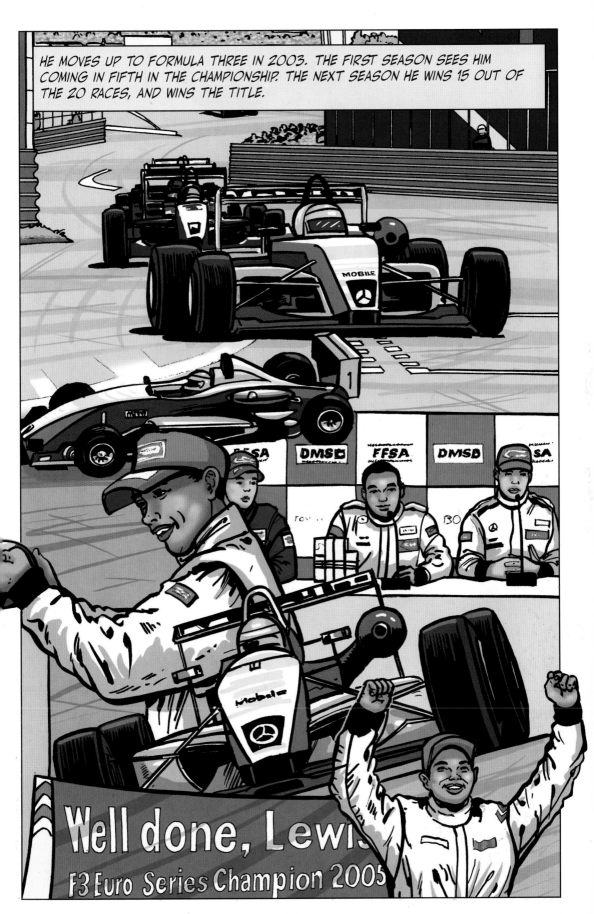

HE MOVES UP TO FORMULA THREE IN 2003. THE FIRST SEASON SEES HIM COMING IN FIFTH IN THE CHAMPIONSHIP. THE NEXT SEASON HE WINS 15 OUT OF THE 20 RACES, AND WINS THE TITLE.

Well done, Lewis
F3 Euro Series Champion 2005

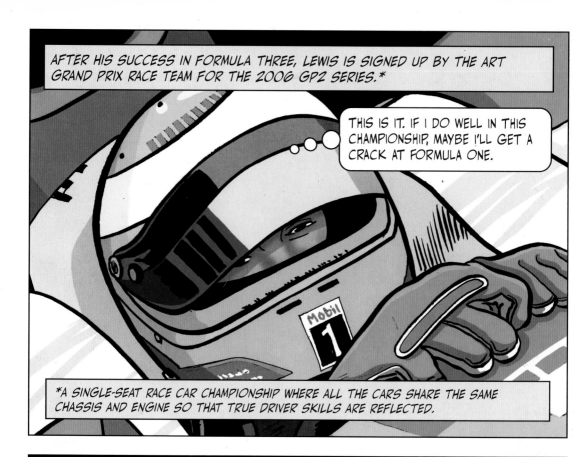

AFTER HIS SUCCESS IN FORMULA THREE, LEWIS IS SIGNED UP BY THE ART GRAND PRIX RACE TEAM FOR THE 2006 GP2 SERIES.*

THIS IS IT. IF I DO WELL IN THIS CHAMPIONSHIP, MAYBE I'LL GET A CRACK AT FORMULA ONE.

*A SINGLE-SEAT RACE CAR CHAMPIONSHIP WHERE ALL THE CARS SHARE THE SAME CHASSIS AND ENGINE SO THAT TRUE DRIVER SKILLS ARE REFLECTED.

AT THE BRITISH GP2 RACE, AT SILVERSTONE, LEWIS'S SKILLS ARE IMPRESSIVE.

PIQUET AROUND THE OUTSIDE OF PICCHIONE...

AND HERE COMES HAMILTON. THEY ARE THREE WIDE INTO MAGGOTS.

IT'S NOT GOING TO WORK.

YES IT IS.

AND HAMILTON LEADS.

MUCH TO HIS FATHER'S JOY, LEWIS GOES ON TO WIN THE RACE AND THE CHAMPIONSHIP.

IN NOVEMBER 2006, LEWIS'S DREAM OF BECOMING A FORMULA ONE RACE CAR DRIVER COMES TRUE...

THE FORMULA ONE MCLAREN-MERCEDES TEAM HAS ANNOUNCED TODAY THE SIGNING OF TWENTY-ONE-YEAR-OLD LEWIS HAMILTON.

IN HIS FIRST RACE IN FORMULA ONE, IN MELBOURNE, AUSTRALIA, LEWIS GETS A PODIUM POSITION BY FINISHING THIRD. BY THE END OF THE FOURTH RACE, IN SPAIN, HE HAS FOUR PODIUM FINISHES AND IS, INCREDIBLY, LEADING THE CHAMPIONSHIP.

AT THE BEGINNING OF THE SIXTH RACE, IN CANADA, LEWIS IS ON POLE POSITION FOR THE FIRST TIME.

HE BUILDS UP A 20-SECOND LEAD, BUT WHEN KUBICA CRASHES, THE SAFETY CAR COMES OUT, AND THE REST OF THE CARS CATCH UP WITH HIM.

LEWIS STAYS COOL AND REMAINS IN FRONT. THE SAFETY CAR IS DEPLOYED A SECOND TIME, AND AGAIN THE REST OF THE FIELD CATCHES UP...

"THE ROOKIE DRIVER, LEWIS HAMILTON WINS HIS FIRST GRAND PRIX."

BUT HE IS JUST TOO FAST AND GOES ON TO WIN HIS FIRST FORMULA ONE RACE. LEWIS HAMILTON LEADS THE CHAMPIONSHIP UNTIL THE LAST RACE WHEN HIS CAR SUFFERS GEAR PROBLEMS, AND HE MISSES WINNING THE 2007 CHAMPIONSHIP BY A SINGLE POINT.

THE END

HOW TO BECOME A RACE CAR DRIVER

The world of race car driving is extremely competitive. Only the best will get to race cars.

FIRST THINGS FIRST

The first thing you should do is read as much as possible about the sport. Also, try to get to meet and talk with the people involved in the sport. From mechanics to drivers, they will all have valuable information to help you on your way to that ultimate goal. A good way to meet these people is to go to racetracks and if possible get a pit pass. Try volunteering for jobs such as selling tickets or ushering. After that try to get onto a race team. Offer to wash engines or polish the race car. Do whatever you can, and talk to as many people as possible. The more you hang around race circuits the more you will learn.

EARLY RACING

You can never be too young to start racing. Many of today's champions started racing karts at a very early age–Lewis Hamilton started racing at the age of eight. There are many local karting organizations, as well as the World Karting Association (WKA), which can supply information on training and race events. There are also racing schools, many of which can be found on the internet at www.racingschools.com. Learning to race can be very expensive. Besides the cost of the racing machine, there are the costs of maintenance and transportation to the racing meetings. If drivers show promise, they may attract a sponsor who will carry part or all of the costs.

GLOSSARY

aggressive Pursuing something forcefully.

aluminum alloys Lightweight metals that are a mix of aluminum and another metal such as copper, zinc manganese, silicon, or magnesium.

chassis A car's frame, on which the engine and other parts are fixed.

clavicle Collarbone.

formula The classification of a race car, usually by engine size.

inevitable Certain to happen.

maintenance The process of keeping something in good condition.

modify To change something.

pits The part of a racetrack where the race car is garaged and where teams can change tires and refuel the car.

podium The raised platform where the winner, second-place, and third-place drivers receive their trophies.

primitive Simple or basic.

promote To further the progress of something.

prototype The first working model of a machine (race car).

regulations Rules made by an organization.

sternum The breastbone.

streamlined Shaped to allow a car to have a small amount of air resistance.

supercharged Supplied with extra power, usually from a mechanical device attached to an engine, such as a turbocharger or supercharger.

tycoon A wealthy, powerful person in business or industry.

variation A difference or change from the norm.

volunteer A person who offers to work for an organization, usually without pay.

FOR MORE INFORMATION

ORGANIZATIONS

World Karting Association
6051 Victory Lane
Concord, NC 28027
(704) 455-1606
Web site: http://www.worldkarting.com

Nevada Vintage Race Car Museum
250 SunPac Ave
Henderson, NV 89015
Web site: http://www.fabulousracers.com/contact_us.html

FOR FURTHER READING

Beck, Paul. *Uncover a Race Car: An Uncover It Book*. San Diego, CA: Silver Dolphin, 2003.

Floca, Brian. *The Racecar Alphabet*. New York, NY: Atheneum/Richard Jackson Books, 2003.

Herzog, Brad. *R is for Race: A Stock Car Alphabet* (Sports). Farmington Hills, MI: Sleeping Bear Press, 2006.

Kelley, K. C. *NASCAR Racing to the Finish*. London, England: Reader's Digest, 2005.

Raby, Philip. *Racing Cars*. Minneapolis, MN: Lerner Publications, 2006.

Wilson, Hugo. *Renault Formula One Motor Racing Book*. London, England: Dorling Kindersley, 2006.

INDEX

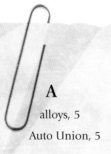

Web Sites

Due to the changing nature of Internet links, Rosen Publishing has developed an online list of Web sites related to the subject of this book. This site is updated regularly. Please use this link to access the list:

http://www.rosenlinks.com/gc/rcdr